CHESHIRE PRIVIES

by

J. BRIAN CURZON

COUNTRYSIDE BOOKS

NEWBURY · BERKSHIRE

First published 1999
© J. Brian Curzon 1999

COUNTRYSIDE BOOKS
3 Catherine Road
Newbury, Berkshire

ISBN 1 85306 593 5

Produced through MRM Associates Ltd., Reading
Printed by Woolnough Bookbinding Ltd., Irthlingborough

CONTENTS

FOREWORD

I felt I knew Cheshire until I was invited to do this research and spent a happy summer during 1998, which was proclaimed to be the warmest in the History of the World. However, in Cheshire it was marked by numerous grey, dull days. I realised that to find the sort of evidence I was looking for I would have to leave the excellent main roads, but in Cheshire it is easy enough. After a turn or two from most busy routes you can be in a long winding lane with rabbits running before you, pheasants strolling by the side or following the ubiquitous black and white cows going home for milking. This is real privy hunting country as those in the towns were usually converted for flushing toilets years ago. The book covers the old county and includes those parts which were given to Merseyside or Greater Manchester during the Local Government changes of 1974.

It often seemed like a safari in search of a rare animal. Privies are a vanishing species in Cheshire and elsewhere, hence the publisher's aim to produce a volume on each county. Most are converted to other purposes – though I found two still in use. Many, with or without their seating arrangements, are used as tidy garden sheds or fuel stores. Ralph Warburton of Buerton invited me to see a two-seater built for an old farmyard. It is used as a summerhouse at the end of a winding path with a pergola of roses. Its two hinged seats are intact and it forms a charming and romantic bower. I lifted one of the lids and resting inside was a dusty champagne glass! It could only occur in Cheshire – that was real class!

Often I had difficulties convincing a householder that their little building was previously a privy. Only once, however, was access refused – by an elderly lady living alone in a country cottage who could not believe that I wanted to put her privy in a book. Once, at Huxley, I was reported to the police who followed up the matter (wasting a lot of time on a Bank Holiday Monday) because someone saw me take a photo of former privies at the rear of a row of houses! I showed the young policeman who visited me another book in the series. I will always remember his stern look as he asked, 'What are privies?' followed by a smile and a blush as he turned the pages and realised what the subject was.

Just like a wild animal, privies can be well camouflaged. I took several photos of privies in pretty gardens or festooned with climbing plants, only to realise that by the time the picture was reproduced in the book people would only see the plants. At other times when I investigated what looked like a promising little roof it turned out to be a porch, a roof over a garden gate and even a small bus shelter seen from a distance. I was often informed that I had come too late. People told how the privy seat had been removed to make a store or how the 'little house' had been improved with a flushing water closet. For reasons of their architectural interest I have included photos of the exteriors of several privies which these days have nothing historic inside.

In some parts of the county, especially in the north of the old shire along the Mersey from the Wirral to the Longendale, most of the housing is 19th and 20th century and the towns were amongst the first to adopt sewers, admittedly not always good ones. The gridiron plan with back alleys was designed for easy emptying of privies but was readily adapted when the sewers were installed so they were amongst the first working class houses to have outside flushing facilities.

Even in single track country lanes in parts of Cheshire there are large modern houses in huge gardens lining the road. Ever since the 19th century Cheshire has been a place to set up ideal homes for people working in the surrounding cities and industrial towns and it is known as the best heeled of the shire counties with more millionaires and Rolls Royces (made at Crewe) per square mile than anywhere else on earth. One thing that an ideal home-owner does not want in the garden is an outside lavatory – especially an unflushable one. Today houses which were built for farm labourers are the homes of commuters who have seen the old privy and outbuildings demolished to be replaced by landscaped gardens and the double (or bigger) garage which is apparently absolutely essential for rural living these days. More than one former privy now houses the children's pony. Outside Tushingham's delightful Blue Bell Inn (noted for its story of a ghostly duck in a bottle) it is a pretty home for a pet sheep.

I must thank various people for their help, all those who allowed me access to their property and sent me their stories. I have tried to include extracts from as many as possible, but often the same sort of story was told by several people. I took hundreds of photos and only a selection of the locations I visited could be included. Especial thanks go to Glenys and Colin Walsh with Nick Hughes for services 'in loo'. Most local papers published appeals for stories and they came in from all parts of the county, funny and touching. I shared someone's memories most mornings when the post arrived and I am grateful for them all.

I remember how my mother would often tell me how she would do her homework in the privy by the light of a candle. When she passed the exam to go to the Technical School her father told her if they could not teach her at school she should not bring work home – a common enough sentiment in the days when parents believed children should be earning not learning. She found the quiet of the privy a help to concentration. I wonder what she would have made of the subject of this book? I think she might have been shocked by some of the words for which there are no replacements and I was reminded of the song:

> Good authors now, who once knew better words,
> Now only use four letter words,
> Writing prose – anything goes.

I have long been involved in archaeology, going back to the first dig I organised in Roman Northwich in 1967, and I jokingly promised to write a book about the history of lavatories after we excavated several medieval cesspits in Cheshire. When we worked on the moated site at Marton Grange in 1970 there was a little privy in a lean-to next to an old potting shed. It had an old 'wee-board' with two holes. We put a plastic bucket with some Elsan fluid in it for the excavators to use but the boys objected to the smell – they preferred to go behind the privy and keep the water level in the moat replenished. I went to photograph it when I started to write this book but found that the island had been used for free range pigs who had broken the seat down. Pigs have no sense of heritage!

I am convinced that the study of privies is an important, but sadly neglected aspect of social history and originally termed the project 'a lavatorial history of Cheshire', but my sarcastic friends (who refused to be photographed demonstrating any of the items featured) soon started to call this research 'Brian's Crap Book'. Here, then, is the nearest thing I will ever write to a 'dirty book'. I hope you enjoy reading it as much I enjoyed the preparation.

J. BRIAN CURZON

In the absence of a loo roll, the author was handed a copy of the day's newspaper. (Photo courtesy of George Twigg).

[1]

AN AGE OF INCONVENIENCE

It seems unbelievable that the need for the modern toilet and bathroom is so recent. There has been some form of human life for at least 2 million years but efficient flushing toilets only became common towards the end of the 19th century and indoor bathrooms for ordinary people were not general until the second half of the 20th century.

It was only when groups of people started to live together in large numbers that finding a 'place to go' became essential. In rural peasant economies men would spend most of the day in the fields or at rural crafts and would simply go to one side and do what had to be done. Women stayed around the home but in the countryside they too would find it easy enough to pop outside with no specific provision – who has not done the same on country walks?

The oldest excavated settlements in Cheshire were built by the Romans. Piped water was laid on to the legionary fortress at Chester (Deva) in AD 79. The famous lead pipes bearing the name of General Agricola, who conquered the north of Britain, show the date by his year of governorship. A section can be seen in the Grosvenor Museum. 'Plumb', the Latin word for lead, gave us the word 'plumbing'. Cleanliness was all important to the Romans. There is nothing in Cheshire to resemble their magnificent communal latrine at Housesteads on Hadrian's Wall but there were efficient stone-lined gutters by the side of the streets within the fortress walls (the word 'gutter' has the same origin as the digestive system's 'gut'). All sorts of refuse was put into them, and when it rained the water dripped from the eaves directly into them to swill it all down into the river. There were even female deities who presided over the drains.

Deva's soldiers sometimes excavated little squares in the corner of their barrack rooms to the porous sandstone below; they lined them with stone and filled them with gravel to form a primitive urinal. In one barrack excavated on the Deanery Field the neck of a broken amphora (wine jar) had been used to direct all the urine into the same spot.

The medieval Cestrians used the porous sandstone to help drain cesspits. Many objects thrown into them were often wonderfully preserved by the liquid. I was told of a complete periwig found in a cesspit behind a pub – which leaves a lot to the imagination. I once attended a conference on the archaeology of human remains at Chester where a perfectly preserved little pile left by a Viking in York (and specially treated) was passed round for the distinguished scholars to inspect. Scientists have inspected the fillings from such places and discovered remains of the parasites which plagued medieval folk.

There are only two surviving medieval stone castles in Cheshire and both have interesting garderobes. Often people get confused about this word which most glossaries simply describe as 'wardrobe', they think of the modern item of furniture. It was actually a room like a wardrobe in the theatre where clothes were stored, repairs would be done, new garments made and people were helped to dress. Chester Castle formerly had a 'Wardrobe Tower'. A privy in the walls was provided so the bowels and bladder could be emptied before people put on the elaborate and inconvenient upper class costumes. During the day, in informal situations, people would wear loose fitting clothes for convenience when nature called. Little boys wore skirts so they could simply sit down and get on with it until they were old enough to master the complicated art of getting out of adult clothes. In Maoist China young children wore one piece overalls without a seat for the same reason.

The smell of the privy was supposed to keep moths away from the clothes stored next to it. Despite the National Trust shops' reputation for pot pourri and anything with floral scent, in the past people seem to have been largely undisturbed by smells. In an age when people took a bath once a year – 'if they needed it or not' – when all traffic involved horses (with the obvious pollution) and many people lived on farms with cattle, pigs and sheep adding their bit to the layers of filth that covered the paths, a whiff from a privy would have been hardly noticeable. And no one I spoke to about privy-culture in more recent years mentioned using any sort of air freshener. The smell was just a fact of life.

A wardrobe tower was added to Beeston Castle in the 14th century and is the most prominent feature you see when driving up to the entrance. The official guidebook is so coy that it makes no mention of it at all; yet it is one of the most fascinating things to be seen there and gives insights into how medieval people gave consideration to the necessary process. In one wall are two recesses, one a floor above the other. On the outside walls the outlets from the drains can still be seen together in a corner where a pile would build up until someone decided to shift it. What is amazing is that the drain from one is directly above a small window and actually empties through an opening in the centre of the arched top into another hole in the window-sill below! The window would also have had a seat on the sill and so used the same drain! One only hopes that those upstairs ensured that no one was using the one downstairs! It has been suggested that, as the rooms were used as wardrobes, tubs for washing people or clothes were provided near by and periodically tipped down the drains to help cleanse them.

The wardrobe tower at Beeston Castle. The recesses were for privy seats and the middle one drains through the top of the window into the window-sill where there would have been another seat.

There is another window-sill privy at Halton Castle. The inside of the castle is not open to the public but you can find its outlet as it emptied into a natural fissure in the rock. Follow the path to the left of the hotel, find the crack below a window and you can locate the drain by inserting your hand. The rubbish from this was presumably shovelled over the cliff from time to time.

An impressive garderobe tower survives at Brimstage Hall in the Wirral, where the old farm contains shops specialising in art and craft products. I wonder how many people who gracefully sip tea in the garden there realise that the tower once served as a staircase with a privy on each floor for the 14th-century tower house. At the base there is a little door giving access to the bottom of the drains.

When he completed the building of Conway and Caernarvon Castles, Master Walter de Hereford provided masonry at the bottom of the garderobes to stop Welshmen climbing up them to open the gates from the inside. I am not sure if this tells us more about the garderobes or the Welsh! He also left the first public toilets in Britain, in the form of a row of little privies on the town walls at Caernarvon. Walter previously had been employed to design and build Vale Royal Abbey for Edward I and no doubt provided it with excellent toilets and drains for the monks and the masons who worked there. Monastic toilets, termed reredorters (ie behind the dormitory), were served by marvellous stone-lined drains which probably gave rise to the stories of secret passages at so many abbey and other ancient sites. Around Vale Royal there are tales of underground passages that would rival the London Underground, which must derive from discoveries of drains. At Combermere there is said to be one along which the monks went to visit the local pub – a reredorter is more likely. While the one at Stanlow Abbey was said to go to Ince Manor House four miles away.

A loo with a view, the square garderobe drain in a window-sill at Halton Castle.

At Norton Priory near Runcorn the excavated reredorter is clearly visible. It is at the end of the dormitory and refectory (dining room) range and was a large room (perhaps habits were made, washed and stored there too?) with a drain on one side. Above this there would have been a row of wooden seats with a series of holes. The canons lived well regulated lives and would probably all visit together before or after meals. A small brook was diverted to run under the seats to flush them and carry the waste to a mill pool nearby. Another stone-lined drain emptied privies from the 'Chamber in the Forest' (the ancient law courts) on Eddisbury Hill and can still be seen.

The reredorter of Chester Abbey (now the cathedral) was at the east end of the refectory range and fed by water which was piped in from Christleton. Professor Huxley, who defended Darwin in the famous Oxford debate on evolution, decided to look into his ancestry (but not quite so far back as the apes) and found his family originated at that village near Chester. His ancestors had been in dispute with the Abbot about the water and at one time had cut the pipes, leaving the monks without any. He decided it was, perhaps, best not to investigate further. A feature of the Abbey which often causes amusement is the 'lavatorium' next to the refectory. It is a stone shelf on which bowls of water were placed to wash before and after meals. The word lavatory has its origins in the Latin for a bathing pool and indicated washing until this century. Lavender is so called because it was put in laundry and washing water for aroma which acted as an insect repellent. In old records and on the Continent it is the wash bowl, not the water closet, that is termed the lavatory. The word was originally used in the way that people ask if someone wants to wash their hands – implying that they did something else first. To use the bathroom or cloakroom are similar euphemisms.

Handforth Hall had two 'places of easement' as they were politely termed in the 17th century. Probably the most photographed in the county, however, is the one at the entrance to Little Moreton Hall near Congleton, left of the gatehouse. One seat has now been opened up to view but it contained four – two at ground level and two upstairs which had a window for ventilation. At least two other garderobe towers are known to exist at Moreton and when they were excavated recently several 17th and 18th-century chamber pots were found in the pits. They were all broken, leaving us to ponder whether they broke when they dropped in or if

The most photographed privies in Cheshire – at Little Moreton Hall. The small tower to the left of the entrance was built to house four privies which emptied directly into the moat. From an engraving of 1808.

16

they were broken in use and the whole lot was simply shovelled up and deposited. Several examples are on show along with shoes found in the pits – an old tradition to bring luck and fertility was to hide shoes in the house.

In old documents the terms 'closet' and 'close-stool' are often encountered. Both words have the same origins as they could be closed. The stools were usually boxes made of expensive woods with a padded seat under the lid and a bowl in the centre. The medical term 'stools' originated with doctors who examined the content of the stools to diagnose problems. There are two fine ones at Dunham Massey near Altrincham. The inventory of Hugh Starkey of Knights Grange in Winsford records that in 1611 there was a closet containing books. He evidently kept his library in his privy and used his time on the close-stool for reading – a common privy pastime. His wife's contained several small baskets and a workbox, showing it was a room for making and repairing clothes. There was also a close-stool in the attic for the servants.

During the restoration of Churche's Mansion in Nantwich a space was found between the main bedroom and the solar (a well lit room for the women to do needlecraft). It was between the chimney and the wall and interpreted as Margery Churche's closet where clothes could be kept warm and dry. A close-stool and a tub for washing would have been kept there too. Around the county, many architectural features said to be 'priests' hides' were originally privies. The cupboard in the wainscoting at Sandbach Old Hall is too obvious for a hide and was more likely an airing cupboard next to the chimney where chamber pots could be kept until wanted. The cupboard in the King's Room at Dorfold Hall, Acton had a similar purpose with a shelf where wigs and hats could be placed and clothes could hang for the night. There is a square shaft going from top to bottom of the chimney at

A pair of 18th-century close-stools from Dunham Massey; the left is of mahogany and the right one of walnut. (Photo courtesy of the National Trust)

Chorley Hall (Alderley) which has been suggested as a priest's hide. He would have been a very thin priest and certainly cooked when he got out! Another privy drain is more likely.

Royal visits often prompted improved facilities for the 'Royal wee'. At Lyme Park near Disley the yellow rooms were fitted up for a visit by the Duke of York in 1676 and included a small chamber which probably contained the Royal close-stools and served as his wardrobe and dressing room. Not to be outdone, the lady of the house wanted improvements so the ladies of the court would not feel she was inferior. Records survive of payments and specifications to improve 'the height and wideness of Mrs. Legh's closet windows'.

At Norbury Booths near Knutsford we excavated the pit which collected the droppings from a number of privies above it. The tower was of 'Tudor brick' but the pit – around 8 feet by 4 feet – was of stone and was connected to the moat by a short stone-lined tunnel, which would have kept the base clean, as at Moreton. The Knutsford pit went out of use in the Restoration period when it became full of rubbish. Amongst the finds from it was a nearly complete 18th-century chamber pot. I was photographed for the press holding it and my rather straightlaced aunt from Mobberley was outraged that I was holding a 'piss pot' in the posh Wilmslow paper. She was ashamed to tell her neighbours that we were related.

We also excavated a large circular pit next to a medieval house at Swallowcroft in Barnton. It must have been cleaned out from time to time and on the house side a hollowed log was found which acted as the drain from the privy above. A girl called Cecilia – Cess for short – was the obvious choice to work on this. She found Restoration period pottery and took samples from which she extracted oat and barley seeds.

The use of chamber pots goes back to the Middle Ages and an old rhyme survives from the days of the Welsh wars:

Taffy was a Welshman, Taffy was a thief,
Taffy came to my house and stole a piece of beef.
I went to Taffy's house, Taffy was in bed,
So I picked up the 'piss pot' and threw it at his yed.

Many medieval chamber pots were found in the cesspits excavated in Chester. The chamber pot was often a matter to be proud of and was put on display. An 18th-century Earl of Warrington, from Dunham Massey, had several solid silver ones engraved with his coat of arms – one of them was sold by Sotheby's in the 1980s for £10,450. Hogarth's famous print *Night* shows a chamber pot emptied through an upstairs window; the traditional cry of 'gardez l'eau' (beware of water)

Excavating the stone pit at the base of the former latrine tower on the site of
Booths Hall, Knutsford, which went out of use in the Restoration period. It was
flushed by a drain connected to the moat.

is said to be the origin of the term 'loo'. I suspect it was simply that you went to the nearest water and used the posh French word, just as you used the French pronunciation of pot ('po') when referring to a chamber pot. French was the language of manners and delicacy from Norman times. Nurses used to be taught the difference between hyper and hypo by remembering that the po goes under the bed and 'gozunder' is still an alternative name for one.

The old box pews in churches like Warburton and Lower Peover could probably tell a tale or two. Demure guide books simply say that their high backs and doors at the side were to keep out draughts. Sermons then could last a couple of hours and for relief chamber pots and bottles were secreted under the seat for emergency use when the high enclosed pews and voluminous clothes would provide some privacy. Women had a special container called a bourdaloue, named after a clergyman known for long sermons. It had a handle on one end and was shaped so that it could be gripped between the thighs when in use. The main families had their own private pews screened off for privacy – the best surviving is at Woodhey Chapel near Nantwich, where a rattan screen hid them.

However, towns were developing and the authorities were hard pressed to keep the streets clear of 'dunghills', which were probably a mixture of animal droppings and household waste. Dogs and pigs scavenged the streets. The market area at Middlewich was known as 'The King's Mexon' (ie midden – a place where human waste and kitchen rubbish was tipped). The authorities at Nantwich passed a regulation in 1592 that 'Noe inhabitant in this Fee shall set or keep any swynestye or privy within 8 yards of any street or lanes upon fine of 39s. 11d'.

It is uncertain how effective the regulations were, but the stage was set for improvements.

[2]

THE COUNTRY SEAT

I have come to the conclusion that it was the profusion of low cost servants which was mainly responsible for the fact that no one considered finding alternative methods of disposing of the waste until Victorian times. There was always someone around to whisk away the products of the better off behind and so no need to tax the mind on how to improve matters. There were no great advantages in developing water closets until there were adequate drains and these did not become common until the mid Victorian period when cities and towns started to have sewers, as is demonstrated at the Manchester Museum of Science and Industry.

From the 17th century there were chairs with a lift up seat and a container underneath. These, and chamber pots concealed in cupboards, were particularly used after meals when the women withdrew to the withdrawing room and the men stayed around the table. It was not simply to allow the men to indulge in conversation unsuitable for women, but to allow both sexes to make a dash for the chamber pots. A commode in Restoration England was a high lace cap worn by women (from à la mode) but in the 18th century it came to refer to a commodious (spacious) piece of furniture, usually a cabinet or chest of drawers on legs. There is a wonderful collection of them at the Lady Lever Art Gallery in Port Sunlight and they would grace the finest rooms. Often they would contain a chamber pot or two. It was only in Victorian times that the term was used to describe a chair with a chamber pot fitted.

I have been told of a new teacher at one of the poshest schools in Cheshire who burst into laughter when asked to 'Please excuse the girl Honour Kermode'. It obviously sounded very different from that which was intended. As did a Nantwich clothing factory advertisement for 'sewers'.

At Bramall Hall, in a room now used as a store in the Victorian male servants' quarters, I was shown a small urinal like half a bowl screwed to the wall of a cupboard built into the corner. Inside, at waist height, is an inverted pottery cone set into a wooden shelf. There is a tap above it. Its purpose was as a sluice (as in hospital wards) into which the chamber pots could be emptied of liquid and rinsed, then put onto shelves to dry. The solids would be tipped into a privy which must have also been in the room. Mop buckets could also be filled there to clean up any spills.

By and large anyone who was anyone had servants. In Victorian times to employ a servant was the sign that you had entered the middle classes. The working classes had neither the time nor the money to spend on alternatives to 'bucket and chuck it'.

There were many openings in farming communities for those who needed no intellectual ability to empty the pots and pails and do other manual tasks. Children were often coerced to help out too. Margaret Roberts wrote to me of her experiences in Clotton in the 1940s. Her family moved to a cottage with oil lamps, well water and a privy. It was her job each Saturday to dig a trench to empty the bucket. She felt they were very posh as they had two holes and two buckets but only used one. This caused problems when her various aunts visited – at those times it was her job to drain off some of the liquid with an old saucepan and pour it over the hedge, or anywhere out of the way to prevent overflowing.

Mr Jones of Sutton Lane Ends told of his first job at a farm near Rudyard Lake where his very first task was to spread manure over the fields. When this was done he was set to clean out the cesspit in the privy, and took out fourteen barrow-loads of muck, one for each year of his young life. Then he had to swill it out. Despite all this he was not allowed to take a bath and he cycled ten miles home on Sunday for one.

Ken Cross who was born at Earnslow Grange near Sandiway wrote of another group of unfortunates, the seasonal Irish labourers. They came, often returning to the same farm each year, in time for planting the new potatoes and lived in a special little building called a 'bothay' which had a black iron grate by which to keep warm and boil a kettle for hot water. It had rudimentary wooden beds with straw mattresses. One of the first jobs was to give the privies their annual clean out. 'These buildings were constructed in such a way that a large pit or tank was constructed away from the seat to the outside, or backside if you prefer that expression, into which the excreta could gravitate over smooth flagstones at a nice angle to quietly slide into the receiving cesspit.' The contents were wheeled away by the Irish who were quite used to such tasks, 'which wasn't easy with a wooden barrow with a wooden wheel. You can imagine the despair of the pusher when the wheel hit a pothole or stone and his load of liquid and mobile fertility shot from one end of the barrow to the other dealing out some ghastly splashes.' He told of how it was spread around the hazel and pear trees for which Cheshire was well known.

Near Rainow I followed a long lane into the hills, with poppies and snapdragons growing from the dry-stone walls to the little farm and a garden beautifully tended by the Beard brothers. They used their double-seater until the 1960s. It appears to be the last of the old cesspit variety left in

The rear of the splendid privy near Rainow; the door to the double seat is at the level of the top of the steps. A large stone covers the clearing hole – though up to 10 feet could accumulate before there was need to empty it. The shelves above are for pigeons to rest before going in through one of the five holes.

Cheshire, built into a bank. The seating is at garden level and faces the house. To one side a flight of ten steps leads down to the lane behind. A large stone slab covers the access hole, and any liquid would dribble through the gaps to join the cow muck in the lane leading to the shippon. They remember their father using a horse and cart for the occasional emptying. The family could sit in glory above a pile around 10 feet high. In the roof space pigeons would roost to provide a little insulation in cold weather, plus food for the table. At Cross Farm near Sandbach, I was shown a structure with a pigsty at one end, a granary above an open-sided hayshed and a privy at the other end (now with WC).

At Higher Sutton I was shown the two-holed privy that was used by Freda Jones when she was a girl; it had a large hole for adults and a smaller one for children with a stone step

A large scoop used to empty the former cesspit at Cross Farm near Sandbach – the handle is a replacement used for the photo.

leading up to it. The space under the seat was quite shallow and she explained that every so often a man would come with a large metal hoe to pull the droppings out at the end opposite the door – the seating was against the side wall.

To judge by the size of the holes at the rear of Ralph Warburton's two-holer at Buerton it must have been emptied by shovels as they are not big enough for tubs. Bryan Dearden told of a similar one he knew at Oakmere emptied by a shovel. I saw several which I was told had simply been shovelled out from the back, with the contents being spread on the fields. I presume it was Victorian prudery that required somewhere private and enclosed to do such things, rather than the actual method of disposal of the waste, which influenced such buildings. If it was merely shovelled a few yards away from time to time, actually going to the corner of the field would have been more efficient – though more public.

Just when tubs or pails were first introduced in Cheshire is not clear as people never wrote of such things. I have discovered nothing earlier than the 19th century in the county. I only found a few surviving tubs, but all were of a similar nature – around 2 foot high with dustbin-like handles fitted close to the bottom. All were of galvanised iron and looked to be comparatively new by their condition. Early ones were probably coopered tubs, made like barrels from staves, which have long since disintegrated. Some tell of them being carried on shoulders but most accounts describe how two men would carry one between them.

A story from Middlewich, told by Mr Mills, expands on this. The town's tubs were emptied at night by men called nightsoil men, but sometimes more poetically 'midnight mechanics' – the term 'mechanics' was used in the same way as in mechanics' institutes, that is people who did manual work. On one occasion a big, hefty man and a slight, thin

27

man were on duty together. The larger chap got fed up with spills from the awkward dispersal of weight and suggested that he could carry the tubs on his head while the smaller man returned them empty. This went well – their old horse ambling on to each house needing their service – until he picked up one with a rusty bottom and his head went through, showering him in sewage. Word of this got out and as there was a popular song at the time, 'Covered all over in sweet violets', wherever he went people would sing or whistle it after him and he was known as 'Violet' from then on.

In the 19th century the contents of the tubs were put up for tender and one farmer had the contract for Over. He would collect the waste and empty his cart into the old marlpits on his land where it was left to break down. He then sold the stuff to a market gardener from near Little Budworth, who used it on his land and would sell his excellent vegetables from door to door to the people who had unwittingly provided the fertilizer. At other times he would simply open the sluice at the back of his wagon and allow the horse to wander over the fields. His sons were expected to follow and 'litter pick' anything which might be dangerous to grazing animals. All sorts of rubbish ended up in the pails, including drowned vermin and kittens unkindly disposed of there. They even found false teeth occasionally! Sometime afterwards lines of tomato plants would be seen in the fields. As tomatoes were eaten raw the seeds passed through the gut without damage and (well coated with fertilizer) soon sprouted in a hot summer.

The commonest memory was that the tubs were emptied weekly, but Carol Soames told me of her 1940s childhood in Northwich. There was a row of six houses behind the Conservative Club which shared the same privy and it had a huge communal tub, like a dustbin. As so many people used it, the landlord (a builder) sent his men around every night to empty it. There was also a single tin bath which all six houses used in turn, everyone boiling kettles and pans for their neighbours so that it could be topped up as each member of the family followed, one after the other.

Sometimes the tubs got full before the men were due to arrive, causing problems, as was recalled by George Williams who lived in Princess Street, Wharton 80 years ago. There was a field at one end with a stone wall around it and every so often an offensive smell proclaimed that someone had tipped their tub over the wall. George also remembers the nightsoil men coming round as the pubs were closing. They used sawdust to put in the bins to dry them out, before they were returned. He, like many others, remembers the bucket of ashes kept in a corner of the 'petty' and the little shovel used to scatter them into the tub after each use. Like so many people he described 'the shit cart' (I never heard anyone call it anything else) with a large, wide-open top like half a barrel, curving to a round bottom. Several spare tubs hung from hooks on the side. Cyril Morris told me how these were used. He lived in Winsford not far from the sewage works but the privies still had the cesspool under the seating. He always remembered it was a long way down if he fell. The men would come each week, use a long handled scoop to empty the pit and pour the contents into the buckets. These were then passed over the wall to tip into the nearby cart.

From Alan Edwards of Congleton comes the rhyme which says it all:

> Those who use the thunder tub
> Must never stand upon the wood,
> For if, by chance, the wood should snap
> No man on earth will help you back!

[3]

AT YOUR CONVENIENCE

When I started to look for privies I had an image in my mind of what to expect. I remember former privies in town settings which either leaned against a building or were in a group opposite the back door, across the yard along with the coal house and often the wash-house. Later houses, built with piped water laid on, had an outside lavatory at the end of the projection at the rear which contained the kitchen – sometimes with a bathroom above – with the coal house. You can still see such things when exploring back alleys in any

An old privy at the end of a wash-house, photographed in 1891 behind a run down house at Winsford. Victorians were advised to build the privy well away from the pantry.

town or from the elevated position of a train on the Stockport Viaduct or nearing the Runcorn/Widnes Bridge.

When we excavated the Roman site at Castle, Northwich we were allowed the use of two little condemned cottages for tool and finds stores. Neighbours told how, years before, each two-up and two-down had been separated to make four one-up, one-down dwellings. Each contained families with around 15 people. At the back was a single privy for each pair. Over 30 people must have used each one – luckily they had very long gardens where the buckets could be tipped!

I did find a few single unit privies, sometimes free standing and sometimes as a lean-to attached to other buildings. It was interesting to come upon references in old documents and house plans, particularly for the Aston by Sutton Estate, of paired units with matching doors. One was the privy while the other was not the expected coal house but a store to keep the ashes dry for use in the privy.

I found some joined to wash-houses with their typical little chimney from the boiler to identify them. The steam from washing boilers and the smells from privies was the reason for keeping them across the yard and away from houses and the boiling water could be used to swill the privy to sterilise it. A very common group were attached to pig sties. One of the first privies I visited was a well-maintained one near Crewe, which had been in use until a few years ago, when it was replaced by a flushing toilet in a lean-to at the back of the house. It was beautifully scrubbed with its round lift-off lid and pail still in place. I was puzzled by what appeared to be a window or trap door at shoulder height. The owner, Ruby Wood, simply said it was a pigsty, but I did not follow the matter up on that occasion, thinking that one must simply have been built next to the other.

As time went on I heard more and more of the association of privies and pigs. Pig keeping flourished in Cheshire as

31

A wash-house with a chimney and a lean-to privy at one end and water trough at the other in a farmyard at Anderton. Wash houses and privies were usually separated from the house so that steam from one and smells from the other could be kept away from the dwelling place.

they would eat the whey ('curds and whey') left after cheese making. Every rural dwelling, and many in the towns, had a pigsty and some also had dairies. When the pig was killed for the Christmas joint 'you could use everything but the squeal'. Helen Minshull wrote, 'The privy and pig cote were back to back with each other and in the winter it was lovely and warm. You could hear the pigs grunting behind you with only the planks of wood separating the two.' The idea of pigs acting as a heating agent seems quite logical and frequently I found that rural structures were designed as variations on the same theme – luckily the pigs did not object to the smell! The privy was usually furthest from the house so that heavy pig swill could be put in the trough from the kitchen. At about shoulder height in the privy there was a small door giving access to a hen loft above the pigs. Often you would

A self seeded sycamore obscures the entrance to this privy at Bostock, but the hatch to empty the tub can be seen. To the right is the little pig yard and the feeder in which to enter the swill for the trough.

find another hole outside above the pig yard, just large enough for the hens to go in at night where they could roost away from foxes and other animals and lay their eggs. No one actually mentioned collecting eggs this way or clearing the hen droppings through the hatch, which was often quite small. I suppose that you could have cleared muck with a hoe but, that way, would not have collected eggs without breakages. With plenty of children around, however, there would always be one available to do the dirty work.

Often the roof space was used as a pigeon loft. I pointed out the little opening in the gable end of one at Antrobus to a farmer and his helper. 'Nay, they dina train th' pigeons to go in there for a crap did they?' was the bewildered response. I explained that it was where they roosted and laid their eggs. They were not racing pigeons, but were kept to provide eggs and meat for pies – plus acting as insulation by keeping the

A flap in a privy near Runcorn, which gives access to the chicken roost through which droppings were emptied and eggs were removed. Probably a child was tempted to do this with the promise of an egg as a reward.

roof space warm with their body heat. The product of the pigsty, chicken roost, pigeon loft and privy would all be mixed together in a general midden and then be spread upon the fields. They were, in effect, little fertilizer factories.

Many people remember tipping the contents of tubs into pits in the garden. Sometimes a large pit or trough was dug and filled up over the year to be ready for next year's planting; or a new pit was dug each week or two. From Whitegate and Astbury came stories of gardens on which it became dangerous to walk because of the liquid matter not far under the soil! Always the reports were of outstanding vegetables. Rhubarb was particularly associated with privies, and I often found rhubarb plants next to privies where part of a leaf could be torn off if the paper had run out. In mid Cheshire the comic King and Queen Carnival always carried bouquets of rhubarb. I never knew the reason until now.

A pair of substantial privies with pigeon holes above and pigsties behind which served workers' cottages on the Capesthorne Estate. Sometimes the pigeon hole also served as an owl hole, encouraging them to nest and keep down vermin.

Something that I continually came upon is a sort of modesty or privacy screen. A wall would project about a yard from one side of the privy door and then another, at a right angle to it, went in front of the door to make a sort of open-topped passageway along which you would go to pay your visit. I presume that this was so that you could sit with the door wide open for fresh air and no one could see inside. I came upon timber versions and even a screen in attractive golden privet (appropriate for a privy).

Inside, the seating could either face the door, or would be set against the side wall so that there was some screening of your identity when you were sitting. If the tub was emptied from the front there was a wooden door or hatch held in place by wing nuts, but if it was emptied from behind, the

This stone-built privy and ash-shed backs onto the Roman Villa at Eaton by Tarporley; its door is behind an attractive privacy screen of golden privet.

front was usually a solid slab of stone. Everything possible was done to keep the space below the seat insect-free. Lids were sometimes tight-fitting squares, to lift against the wall – though at Eaton by Tarporley I found one that hinged to the side. Otherwise they were movable, either circular or square, and could be set on one side.

At Cotebrook I was invited to see an unusual portable tub container. It had obviously been made since the Second World War, as it was lined with heavy duty polythene – a nice hygienic touch. There was no sign of a previous fixed privy, and it is impossible to tell if this replaced a similar portable one, or if a fixed privy had been replaced with this portable version for the convenience of someone who was often too ill to go down the garden path.

The building material used for a privy reflected the area in

This privy at Eaton by Tarporley must have been awkward to use as the lid lifts sideways; there are solid brick stands under the wood on each side.

which it was built; if there was building stone available it was used for outbuildings, even if brick was used for the house. Slate roofs were most common in brick areas, but in the east the thicker 'Kerridge slabs' were used which made the roof flatter. Helen Minshull writes of a privy 'in a tin and wood shed' at Marton and at Bunbury I came upon what appeared to have been a privy made from railway sleepers set side by side.

Windows were almost always small – for privacy and to retain warmth – though George Twigg's double-seater at Hassal had a large frosted glass window set behind a bushy garden. Most had only a tiny one and often none, or sometimes it was glazed with thick greenish glass that was impossible to see through. At other places a space less than the size of a brick on end was left. Mr Percival of Whitegate still uses his privy and keeps a spare toilet roll stuffed into the

This privy near Crewe was in use until a few years ago when the Council gave a grant to build a flushing toilet. The circular lid is typical and the little door (upper right) gives access to the chicken loft.

The portable privy at Cotebrook in position in a whitewashed sandstone structure at the end of a pigsty.

unglazed slit in it. In times gone by you might stand your candle there so that people could tell it was occupied at night time. Many people remember candles and oil lamps, often left inside to prevent freezing on cold nights when even the pigs and poultry would not be enough to keep them warm. One or two remember the ventilators from the openwork tops of oil stoves making patterns on the roof and walls.

In most privy walls was a small hollow, usually only a few inches square, built into the thickness of the wall but not going all the way through. It was just high enough for a candle or night light held in place with wax but not deep enough for one on a saucer or stick. It is sometimes said that it was where paper was placed, though it would have to be cut into narrow strips to stay there – and most people remember paper on strings. At the side of most privy holes there was plenty of wooden shelf to pile up lots of printed material for reading or cleaning purposes.

Often people would use ashes to cover up the droppings and soak up liquid; it made the pails heavier to carry, but the contents were less smelly and splashy. A box or bucket of ashes was kept in a corner and it was, perhaps, to make room for this that some privies are against the side wall and not the back. Ashes have some nutritional qualities and so would improve the contents of the tubs as a fertilizer for the land.

From 1875 when the first Local Boards of Health were formed, drains were provided in town centres and they took on the job of emptying the tubs and cesspits in undrained parts. Often local farmers contracted to do this work for the councils and to remove horse droppings from the streets. I contacted all the local authorities in the county to enquire if any pail closets were still in use. Only Vale Royal replied, to say that there were six still used in the Borough but they could not disclose by whom or where they were.

40

A nicely preserved single unit privy only a few yards from the M6. The door is set to one side showing that the seat was at the other so that a bucket of ashes could be kept in the corner. Often where the roof has a single pitch it is because there was little need for head-room above the seat.

When Winsford became an overspill development in 1962 the first houses were all provided with outside lavatories as it was felt that the people who came from Manchester and Liverpool would not know about inside facilities. Frank Sumner was one of the newcomers who was given a job with the Council. He found, to his dismay, that it was on the wagon which emptied the local privies. His companion felt it was a good job because no one was supervising and he was content to eat his sandwiches as the cart was drained into a sewer near the filter-beds. After a month Frank was totally downhearted and begged to be given another job – or he would go back to Liverpool.

Ruth Ashe has happy memories of her Grandma Kent who lived in Swettenham Street, Macclesfield, in one of a short terraced row of houses which shared a single flushing toilet. The key to the lavatory was kept on a string with a bobbin and to reach it she had to go through four gates and be sure to shut them after her. This 'was quite a luxurious affair when compared to the facilities available at the home of Grandma Birchenall. Here the privy was a bleached white seat stretched across the width of the whitewashed brick outhouse. In the centre was a round hole with a central knob for lifting. On one wall hung a neat wad of newspaper squares suspended on a piece of string. Below the wooden door was a gap of some six inches or so and behind the metal latch was a hole which I thought people might peep through whilst I was engaged. Below the toilet there was a raised step which was donkey-stoned by Grandma every week. As a small child I found that climbing onto the seat involved quite an effort and once installed I had a mortal fear of falling through the large aperture into what appeared to be a dark bottomless pit below. With small hands gripping tightly to the seat I would fervently hope that my knickers(at the time suspended around my ankles) would not be too cold when retrieved.'

[4]

THE PLEASURE OF YOUR COMPANY

I found several two-holed privies, but none with more than that. I got word of a three-holer at a farm near Sandbach via a friend who had asked colleagues at work (in the WC factory at Middlewich – where else!). However, the building had been demolished only a few months before, following storm damage in the winter. Sometimes, as in the privy where my mother did her homework and the one I visited at Sutton, there was a smaller hole with a step up to it for the children. On former cheese-producing farms at Haslington and Buerton I saw two-holers that would seat a large farmer and his larger wife with ease – both had tubs, each with its own compartment and strong seat. I was reminded of the comment made about stout women: 'She's built like a brick shit-house!'

The idea of two people sharing so personal an act is strange to modern sanitised minds, but in the past where several shared the same bed and bath (in front of the fire) it seems to have been accepted. The Beard brothers of Rainow told how they would think nothing of popping in together when they returned from the fields. It is a strange anomaly that men will stand next to complete strangers in a public urinal, but will not go in with their friends, while women prefer to go in pairs but sit separately. Freda Jones told how she and her sister would sit for hours with a book each or singing songs in their cosy two seater high in the hills above Sutton.

Some told of how a parent or older sibling would go with little children who might be frightened and it seems to have

A two-seater, now in a poor condition, near Sutton Four Lane Ends where two sisters spent hours reading and singing. It has circular lids which are also slightly damaged but had no tubs; it was emptied from the far end with a large rake.

Garden implements now hang on the wall of this splendid two-seater with hinged lids which was built for a farmer and cheese factor at Haslington. The left door is open to show the galvanised iron tub.

been normal for a child to go with a grown-up while learning what to do. Betty Farday remembers sitting with her granny in a privy halfway down the garden path. 'It was my job to arm her to the loo as she was crippled with rheumatism and was very deaf. There we would sit, side by side, with a rolled up newspaper held to her ear, singing songs. There was a bucket under each seat collected very early Monday morning. A box of riddled ashes complete with the little shovel and squares of newspaper hung on a string.'

An anonymous writer recalled how 'at the Sunday School I attended, the privy was outside. You usually went in pairs and sat side by side with fingers and thumbs pinching the side. Who emptied the cesspit? I have no idea.' Going to such perilous places in pairs must have given some assurance that there was someone on hand to raise the alarm in case of a slip down.

Several people recalled a privy shared with the neighbour, or even a whole row of houses would use the same one. Bertha Moffat told of one at Marston which was a two-holer shared with the people in the next cottage. She did not report if people from both cottages used it at the same time! Each household took it in turns to empty the contents into pits in the garden and keep it clean. Her family provided 'best Typhoo' tea for cyclists who came from as far as Manchester and Liverpool and often there would be a long line waiting to use it before going on their way.

Helen Minshull recalled how she had lived in a cottage in what used to be called 'Ranters Row' because they were all Methodists with a chapel at the end, in Chesterlane, Marton. For five houses there was one privy with two holes, one bigger than the other. 'Old Mr Mathers and Mr Vernon spent many hours reading the newspapers there and often you shared a seat. We took it in turns to keep it spotless.' She, too, remembers providing tea for cyclists, which was a popular thing for country people to do to make a few bob between the wars. Before cars became common, town people would take their bikes on the train to country stations for a ride, often returning via another station. They welcomed the chance to sit for a drink and have use of the privy if they were in mixed sex groups – cyclists were often teetotallers and avoided pubs. The Manchester writer Fletcher Moss told how he could not get a cup of tea in Cheshire around 1900 on hot days when he travelled by bike, because pubs did not light a fire to boil a kettle.

There was sometimes separation of classes, a real 'mire-archy'. In large country houses the family had their facilities inside emptied by servants who had their own privy outside. At the Aston by Sutton Estate yard there was a pair of two seaters with tubs, back to back, connected by a small door (which suggests that one side was formerly a pig and hen cote). On one side the ordinary workmen had a scrubbed deal seat, in the other the senior gardeners had a mahogany seat (possibly moved out of the house during alterations) while nearby was a single unit just for the head gardener. At the workhouse in Northwich the Guardians had a splendid inside toilet, surrounded by mahogany. The 'throne' and wash basin were of beautifully blue and white transfer-printed porcelain. The inmates had tubs in a row of outside privies with the ash-pit next to it so that there was a supply for the bucket.

Hilda Thompson, aged 82, was the only one to mention sharing with the opposite sex when she recalled going for a walk with a friend through Romiley and Marple as a 16 year old. 'Opposite to Ludworth Primary School a lady in a cottage made us a cup of tea. I asked if she had a toilet and she said "round the back" I went round, there was a shed with

In this neglected structure at Aston by Sutton the pig yard is to the left. The roof of the former pig cote with hen cote above is in the centre and the door to empty the privy tub can be seen on the right.

no front. There was a plank with two holes, I sat on one and a boy of about 7 years old came and sat on the other. I said "where's the toilet paper?" He said "I'll ask me mam." He came back and said "This is all she 'ad" and gave me a piece of newspaper.'

A small sheaf of amusing tales arrived one morning from 'Henry of Chester'. It included the story of an aunt visiting with a new posh handbag, of which she was very proud, and she would not let it out of her sight, even when she went to the privy after dark. She returned in a terrible state, repeating 'You might have told me!' Since she had last visited an increase in the family had caused the former one-holer to be upgraded to a two-holer. She had carefully put her bag next to her and it had fallen down the new hole.

The canal boat people had little chamber pots which (like everything else in their tiny cabins) were stored out of sight. You can see examples at the Boat Museum in Ellesmere Port where, behind a row of workers' cottages, there is also a preserved privy complete with newspaper on string and a dummy of an old boatee deep in contemplation. Today canal cruisers have special tanks with which to flush. At Anderton all the boats are named after famous artists and the vessel that empties the tanks is named Twoloos Lautrec.

However things were not so sanitised and clinical in the past as the chant of Middlewich children shows:-

> Boatee, boatee, shit in the cut, shit in the cut, shit in the cut,
> Boatee, boatee, shit in the cut and wipe your arse on a mop stick.

[5]

THOUGHTS ON PAPER

I remember using squares of newspaper as a child – as do so many others – and even in adult life when I have run out of toilet roll I have thrown a newspaper into the bathroom to tear bits off until I remembered to buy replacement rolls. When stuck in a public loo with no paper I have searched through my pockets for old receipts or other paper scraps and once in despair actually used a cheque torn from my cheque book! I was tempted to make it out for a million pounds but, caught short, I stopped short!

Specially made toilet paper only became available in the 1870s and before that anything to hand would be used. A couple from Nantwich took part in a TV experiment in the 1970s by joining others to live in a reconstruction of an Iron Age hut. They dug a cesspit and hung leaves to act as toilet paper. Few country dwellers have not looked for dock leaves or long grass to do the same when away from dwellings.

The Roman soldiers used sponges on sticks in their super-loo at Housesteads fort and washed them in running water in a channel in front of them. Monks in the Middle Ages often used old habits (robes) cut into pieces and washed out. Other people used sphagnum moss and it is now known that this contains a mild antiseptic and so was particularly appropriate. A 1617 map of the Vale Royal estate shows 'Wet Arse Moss' near to the old abbey which tells its own tale. If James I, who visited Vale Royal that year made use of it is not recorded. The use of wet cloths is the origin of our term 'toilet', for 'textoilet' was once a particularly soft fabric favoured for washing-cloths. The bidet is not a new idea and

A selection of lavatorial items from the 1888 Twyford's catalogue included
bidets, pots to fit in commodes, bed pans and urinal bottles.

Victorian catalogues for the Twyford's company illustrate them. There is one in their museum at Alsager which is vaguely hourglass in outline and set into a wooden stool. It held warm water and a cloth or sponge.

Other alternatives to newspaper such as mail order catalogues were sometimes put in the privy, and many people remember starting to read something while waiting to use the paper only to find the end of the item had already been used. Our term 'bumph' for junk mail implies that it was only good enough for toilet use in the past – though today it is usually a bit too slippy and shiny. At Eaton by Tarporley I found a nice wooden file built into the door so that newspapers could be kept tidily. Was this to keep paper away from candles and lamps as fire prevention? Bryan Dearden joked about the newspapers in his privy saying that the potatoes from the garden came 'ready wrapped in the *Daily Express*'. It is said that visitors to Buckingham Palace often remarked that 'One would think the Empress of India could afford toilet paper' as Queen Victoria had sheets cut from *The Times*. In the Twyford's museum are a couple of stands made of glazed pottery in which the cut sheets of paper could be placed neatly to go with their elegant flushing toilets. Their old catalogues show them behind the seat on the fixed wooden part and fitted around the pipe. In the most elegant houses the paper was cut with 'pinking shears'.

Some remember the luxury of using the tissue from round an orange or apple – particularly at Christmastime. I have been told of children sent to scavenge for boxes to use as firewood when the local market closed down for the day who would stuff one box full of fruit tissues for the petty.

The old Izal and Bronco brands of toilet tissue were best for pail closets as softer tissue made a gungy mess. They were especially used in places such as pubs, public conveniences and schools. We always called our Geography teacher 'Bog

This wooden file on the back of a privy door at Eaton by Tarporley was for newspapers – before the toilet roll holder above was fitted.

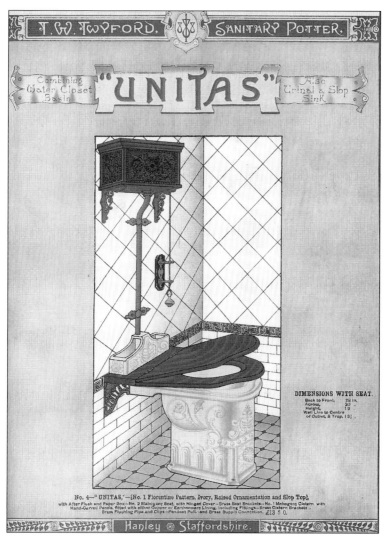

The height of Victorian elegance. Twyford's Unitas in a tiled room with Florentine decoration on the closet and hand-carved wooden covers for the pottery cistern. A container for cut up newspaper is at the back. Items like this are now treasures of the company museum at Alsager.

House Bertha' as she regularly arrived with a handful of the stuff. It was more efficient as tracing paper for maps than what it was made for!

I once heard of one young girl who refused to use the 'recycled' toilet roll her mother had purchased because she presumed that it had already been used and was washed somehow for reuse!

There were other alternatives. The investigations into the water supply for Northwich in 1885 looked into using water from Wade Brook to supply drinking and washing water. A ditch behind Jabez Thompson's Brick Works at Lostock drained into the brook. This was described as 'a common privy' and was full of scraps of paper. It appeared that workmen on the railway used the ditch for the same purpose as there were also considerable quantities of cotton waste which they used instead of paper. This was used in the cotton mills too and would be much softer, let alone more efficient, than newsprint. Old rags were also often used and the Northwich Rural District Council's 1951 handbook for tenants advised people moving into a new house, who were not familiar with flushing toilets, not to use rags and put them into the drains where they could cause blockages or they would be charged to clear them!

[6]

FRAGRANT MEMORIES

My brother remembers using one of these privies at Tarporley – which had a cess pit under the seat – when visiting an aunt during the Second World War. The left is of brick with a door to empty the tubs, and the right is of sandstone with a tiny ventilation slit under the roof.

People had more tales to share with me than those about simply sitting on the seats and emptying the results.

Alan Edwards wrote that he was 'born in a room where a murder was committed, an attempted murder and a suicide. My people moved in afterwards in 1880. It was at the Brownslow Arms near Astbury and the previous landlord, who was called Bracegirdle, shot his wife, wounded the bailiff who was waiting outside and then turned the gun on himself.

There were marks on the tap-room ceiling which were said to be the bloodstains . . . Charabancs from the Potteries, Manchester and Stockport arrived each weekend full of people eager to see the infamous bloodstains. The pub did well, but so did the rhubarb – it threatened to blot out the sun. The toilets were three or four thunder-tubs and on busy bank holidays Dad had to dig more trenches than he did on the Somme. If you took a stroll in the vegetable patch you had a sensation of being at sea as the ground pitched and rolled with each step. Something had to be done. Dad dug a hole and filled it with clinker and with a bit of plumbing had the first water closets in the village.' On the cement were written the heartfelt words 'Thank God for this'.

Another tale of a home-made filtration came from Don Sant of Moulton. His grandparents lived in a cottage near the old Hartford Bridge where the privy with pails was converted to a sort of septic tank arrangement filled with basses from the Newbridge Salt Works. Basses were the residue left after burning poor quality coal and made good filters for such purposes. He went to work at Vale Royal House in a little rowing boat and would bring fresh supplies of basses from the salt works in the boat.

Ken Bentley told me how he took his new wife to visit a friend in a cottage on the Arley Estate at Aston by Budworth. She asked where the toilet was and came back from her visit to the bottom of the garden looking agitated. He did not realise that she had discovered that there was an old 'thunder box' privy there. She suddenly started to suggest that they would have to leave so that she could get cigarettes from the Red Lion at Pickmere. When they arrived she made a dash for the ladies. She had been disgusted at the cottage privy and afraid to go inside in case there were spiders.

Behind one of Cheshire's quaintest pubs, the Blue Bell at Tushingham, the former privy has been painted black and white to match the pub and is now the home of a friendly sheep.

TALES OF THE TIPPLER

From near Duckinfield Louisa Roe wrote, 'Our toilet was made of pot, brown in colour, with a wooden seat. I remember one day my mum was beating the carpet on the line and I was screaming my head off because my kitten 'Tiddles' had fallen down the lavy. I knew that if the stone at the bottom turned over my kitten would be lost for ever. Mum ran over with her yard brush and slowly put it down the lavy. I don't know how she managed it but my kitten was hanging on the brush head for dear life as she brought it up. I always remembered, after that, to shut the lavy door!'

She was talking about what I discovered was a 'Duckett's Patent slop water closet' when I photographed one behind a house dated 1902 in Knutsford. Water was held a few feet under the metal cover in front of the seat until there was

A Duckett (as a change from a bucket) photographed in Knutsford. The mopstick (right) could be used in an emergency to flush the 'long drop' under the seat. The metal cover could be lifted to remove anything which prevented the tipper from tipping.

sufficient weight to tip the 'tippler' and wash out the drain. The tipping device – known as the stone because it was stoneware – could also be sited under a grid in the yard where access was easy to clean it if rubbish got in and stopped it working.

It was invented in Burnley (where I once encountered one) by the appropriately named G.H. Pickles, a civil engineer for the Corporation (his name was almost as apt as that of Thomas Crapper, the famous 19th-century refiner of the cistern), manufactured by Duckett's of Burnley who took out the patent in 1887. Mr Kilgannon wrote from Hyde of a house he had lived in just after the war which had one he knew as a 'tipperly'. It was a special section of drain like a box in which something resembling the tipping part of a dumper truck was suspended on short round arms. There is a working example on show at the Manchester Science Museum. All the water from the house and rainwater from the down-spouts ran into this along the drain where it was stored. The privy, further along, 'had a wooden seat over a sort of funnel so that everything dropped into the drain below' where a small quantity of water was held in a U trap. As the water filled the tank it tipped up sending sufficient force to move the droppings into the main drain. You could use a mop-stick or brush handle to empty the tippler before it was full.

A writer who simply addressed the letter 'Looking Back' told of another Duckett with a hole 5 or 6 feet deep and flushed by a tippler. 'On dark nights before going up to bed it was my older brother's duty to take his little sister to the toilet. Candle in hand he would carefully hide a newspaper under his jacket, prop the candle in the corner, light the newspaper with it and drop it down the loo. He would say, 'sit on it quick, it will warm your bum.' She told how her grandmother 'was an avid reader of *The Red Letter* which was running a serial about Maria and the Red Barn. She used to put the magazine under a cushion, but I could always find a way to take it to the toilet and find out what naughty Maria was doing in that Red Barn!'

BOYS WILL BE BOYS

Many people remembered pranks in the toilet. Ruth Ashe told of how rude boys at her school would pull out the bins from the little doors which backed into a yard behind and look up. 'On one occasion some very naughty boys set fire to a pile of old newspaper and placed it under the seat when it was being used by teacher, Miss Duckworth, I can hear her screams today but I don't think she ever caught the culprits.'

Gwyneth Whalley recalled her childhood privy which she was terrified she would fall into, and of how her parents referred to the men who emptied it as 'gentlemen of the night'. She started school at Wharton Infants which had what could be described as automatic flushing lavatories, where a general open drain ran under all the seats to cleanse them at intervals. The girls and boys sat back to back and one of the boys realised that if he put his head down the hole he could see a row of little bottoms in the girls' side. Julie Heath told of how the toilets at her infants school in Weaverham had been updated from the communal flushing variety to individual water closets. However, they were still roofless as they were built to let smells escape. Finding seats wet after rain or covered with snow was a regular occurrence.

The lads' pranks on the farm where he grew up on the Vale Royal Estate were remembered by Ken Cross. His sisters and a governess would be tickled or nettled as they paid their call. At Antrobus I was told about an enamel bowl which just fitted into the hole in the privy seat. On dark nights the boys in the family would put the bowl, filled with cold water, in the hole then watch for one of their sisters to come out when they had finished washing up after the meals and listen for the squeals when she sat in the water.

A builder's yard at Alderley, where there were open-topped drains to use as a urinal which then passed under a row of compartments with wooden holes cut through the continuous plank, was a vivid memory for George Twigg. A little boat would be made from wood and a rag soaked in paraffin was placed in the open drain to float under the exposed rears of those in the compartments. I never heard of women playing tricks on men!

NEIGHBOURLY ACTS

My correspondent 'Henry of Chester' wrote of how the fireman on one of the railway engines coming out of a chemical works at Runcorn would work the night shift and push some coal from the tender as it passed along an embankment to the rear of his house. One night he dislodged a very large piece of coal which rumbled down the bank with some force, crashing through the back of a privy where his neighbour's wife was sitting. To calm matters they apparently agreed that in future they would share the coal. From the same works full strength bleach could be purchased by employees for very little cost and a neighbour poured loads of the bleach into the outside toilet every time it was used. One Sunday her husband, who was a big man, went in to use it in his Sunday-best suit and the seat collapsed into a pile of sand and gravel. The bleach had penetrated through old cracked glaze to eat away at the very structure. Needless to say the suit was ruined.

A phone call from a lady who lived near Crewe shed some more light on housing conditions between the wars. She remembered living in the middle house of three. Her grandfather lived at the end and the tubs were emptied by the nightsoil men who came around the end of the row and through his yard. When he died, a new tenant moved in and fenced off the access. From then on the tubs had to be carried through the kitchen and parlour to the front door each week and coal had to be delivered the same way. They were pleased when their father got another job and they moved to a house with running water and a flushing toilet. It was to prevent such incidents that Housing Acts insisted that terraced houses should be provided with entries and that breaks were provided at specified distances for access and to stop fires spreading.

OF JERRIES AND GOZUNDERS

Few people had stories of chamber pots, though Louisa Roe remembered that 'if you forgot to put it back under the bed you ended up with wet, smelly feet. Our "jerry" broke and Mum made us use a bucket, which wasn't half hard on the backside. I knocked it over many a time. Mum showed me the stains on the downstairs ceiling; "There," she'd say, "now I've got to find some whitewash to try and clean up the mess."'

I was told of a group of young men who were in lodgings where there was an outside privy, but they had a chamber pot in their room. One night after a long session at the pub it became embarrassingly full and they still needed to use it. One of them opened the window to tip some liquid out, but knocked and broke it while putting it through, and he was left holding nothing but the handle. All looked thoroughly ashamed of themselves when they confessed to the landlady the next day.

When I was a child and we went carolling or souling (singing the traditional begging song at the start of November) older people would warn us to beware in case someone tipped the jerry on us. No one ever did, thankfully. The term 'jerry' for a chamber pot goes back at least to the 18th century and its resemblance to a German helmet is coincidental. Outside lavatories were known as 'the Jerichos' because of the noise of trumpeting which sometimes emerged from them.

I worked part-time at the Crown Hotel in Northwich in the 1970s and one day when workmen had to go into the attic to do some repairs we seized the chance to take a look. A large Victorian 'gozunder' (chamber pot) was in a corner and I decided to take it home as it might come in handy on a cold night. Jean, the cook, rinsed years of dust off it and turned round with a sense of awe to announce 'Lawrence of Arabia might have used that!' There was a blue transfer proclaiming it came from the Crown and Anchor where he had stayed when working on ship design in Northwich. It was known as 'Lawrence of Arabia's Piss Pot' from then on and found a place of honour in the pub lounge, before vanishing during alterations.

Of course, I had to continue venturing out of my warm bedroom on a chilly winter's night.

A museum guide pays a visit to 'Grandpa' who sits in the preserved privy at the Boat Museum in Ellesmere Port. (Photo *Daily Post*)

[7]

STANDING ROOM ONLY

Nature has designed men and women to function differently in the lavatory. Men usually stand to pass water while women sit – except in Ancient Egypt, where Herodotus tells us it was the other way round! Women have larger bladders and books of etiquette or useful knowledge advised prim Victorian ladies to allow for the fact that their beau might want to excuse himself more frequently than she. On the roof of Witton church at Northwich the difference is made use of in a comic way. A little crouching devil acts as a water spout and when it rains he simply relieves himself. At one time it poured away from the wall in a stream resembling the Brussels Manneken Pis but now it has been sanitised by the addition of a drain to act as a loo.

Medieval advice includes 'beware of emptying pysse pottes and pyssing in chimnes'. This referred to the hearths (rather than the chimney) where the liquid would evaporate or drain into the ashes. This was unlikely to be a problem in pre-Jacobean Cheshire where Daniel King in 1656 recorded that:

> Till of late years they used the old manner of the Saxons, for they had their hearth against a hob of clay and their oxen also under the same roof but within these 40 years it is altogether altered, for they have builded chimnies and furnished other parts of their houses accordingly.

I guess that people simply went to the animal end of the building and added their own little pile to theirs!

Standing Room with a view. These urinals are hardly more than waist high to an adult and are behind the old school at Moore near Runcorn. Little boys probably tried to outdo each other at the ancient art of peeing over the wall – jokingly said to be the origin of the Cheshire village name Peover.

Urine was a useful commodity and the Romans provided tanks in the street for those who could oblige. Some of the jugs – especially tall, narrow ones – found in medieval cesspits in Chester were probably used to collect urine overnight. It was an important ingredient in saltpetre factories (and so got back into the food chain when employed in curing meat). In addition the ammonia in it helped not only to remove greasy food stains from clothing but also to bleach new fabrics. Mature male urine was a useful fixative for dyestuffs, where the hormones provided subtle colour changes. Some stalwart hand-spinners still experiment with it. An anonymous writer recalled how she was told by her mother, in the 1920s, that the strange smell encountered when washing blankets was because the manufacturer soaked them in urine. In Pennine villages there were 'lant troughs', rather like a stone box with a little roof to keep leaves and other debris out of the tub it contained, to collect the locals' urine, which was termed 'lant' in the textile trades. There is a good example in Wycoller Country Park in Lancashire. I was told that Stockport Library had saved one of the last mobile lant troughs used in the Borough to put on display many years ago – but unfortunately neither the library nor the museum had any knowledge of it.

I wonder how many people in Knutsford realise that before their parish church was built in 1745 the area was the 'tenterfield' where newly bleached or dyed fabrics were hung out on tenter-hooks to dry and to let the ultra violet of the sun react with the urine in the fabric to bleach or colour the cloth. The surnames Walker and Fuller derive from people employed to walk on the cloth to force the urine into it.

Opposite the churchyard gate in the Bottom Street (how appropriate) in Knutsford is a corner where two adjoining

67

buildings had slightly different frontages. This has been bricked up to discourage people from using it as an impromptu urinal. Once you know what to look for you see other devices used for the same purpose, such as a large glacial erratic boulder put in a tempting nook. On the front of the Weaver Navigation Offices in Northwich there is an iron fence preventing access to an inset corner. A specially made iron bracket keeps people away from a similar spot behind what is now the Heritage Centre at Port Sunlight. Often quarter circles in cast iron, complete with spikes, kept men out of the corners of public buildings. The most vicious of such contraptions I have ever seen was in a back alley in Padiham, Lancashire. It was rather like a quarter of a cast-iron umbrella – designed to pour the liquid back over the clogs of those who dared use it.

There was another commercial use for urine in Cheshire, in the many salt works, where urine was passed directly into the

A fenced-off corner of the Weaver Navigation Offices in Northwich. This device prevented men using it as an emergency urinal.

pans of boiling brine to prevent frothing and to help produce certain grades. The intense heat would kill any germs in it. This was one of the reasons women were banned from working near the salt pans by law. The exact details of how and when to do it are lost as no salt is made this way any more and public health officials would be outraged at the idea. The use of urine still continues in some traditional salt works abroad and may well be in the fancy varieties sold by health shops. The use is very ancient and it is possible that a large round amphora (wine jar) found set into the ground by a salt furnace excavated near King Street, Middlewich and now on show in the Town Library was used to collect urine for this reason. The word 'AMURCA' is on it, translated as 'salty waste'. As the salt works were usually by a river or canal

A drawing of a salt works privy at Meadow Bank, Winsford, by Tom Lightfoot, a former boatman and salt worker whose memories and drawings are kept at the Lion Salt Works, Marston.

to provide transport for the coal and the salt, disposing of excess contents into them was a simple procedure.

Men and boys were encouraged to use grids in corners, particularly those in the backyards in towns, which were kept flushed by the drains from the roof and the wash-house sink. They were encouraged to simply find a decent spot to pass water onto the plants – keeping them watered in summer; apparently it was a good nutrient too. This avoided overfilling the tubs so that they overflowed. Adult men would also use the shallow brown slopstone in the wash-house. They were not used like the kitchen sink, as washing up was done in enamel bowls in the back kitchen, but washing water, buckets used for mopping and scrubbing, and the liquid from chamber pots or from preparing vegetables were all poured into the slopstone to drain away.

However, public decency in Victorian times dictated that there should be a special place for men to go when in need in the town streets. The provision of public toilets for the visitors to the 1851 Great Exhibition led to the introduction of the first penny in the slot machines, for which the price remained the same until decimalisation – hence the term 'spending a penny'. Men refused to pay to sit when they could find a corner to stand in. Simple enclosed 'pissoirs' were provided as a compromise and soon became standard. The name originates from the French for 'ant hill' as that is what they (reportedly) smell like and it is from this that the four letter word is derived.

I don't know if it was a legal requirement but people used to say there was a urinal at about half a mile intervals in the towns. If possible they were placed next to rivers, canals or any convenient watercourse and emptied directly into them. One in Knutsford was over a little brook on a small bridge

A wash-house and privy now used as a garden shed near Audlem. The old slopstone into which chamber pots and waste water were emptied in the past is now used outside as a plant container.

and emptied through the floor. A little lean-to building at the end of a range of outbuildings at the Hare and Hounds, Crowton once contained a privy and a urinal, the liquid from which drained to a tiny brook.

The most unlikely former pub urinal that I came upon was at the Harrington Arms in Gawsworth. I was shown a stairway to a hay store above the milking parlour – it must be the last pub in Cheshire to also function as a farm. The space underneath doubled as a urinal and the liquid ran along a little drain into the grid under the tap which was used for the hose to swill the shippon out.

At the Winsford football stadium there is still a simple wall for privacy and nothing more, the liquid draining into the cinders used to build up a standing area.

Public urinals were usually roofless so that the rain would wash them out – only in recent times did they have flushing

A lean-to gents on the end of a wash-house and store block at the Hare and Hounds, Crowton. The former urinal emptied directly into the brook which runs between the two bollards.

facilities added. Despite keeping an eye open for them in this survey I found that they were even more rare than privies. Not long after Vale Royal Council was established in 1974, a committee of mainly women inspected them all and condemned most of those in the borough as insanitary. Their basic nature and reputation for attracting anti-social behaviour has seen the street corner 'gents' with no seating facilities vanish from the scene in the last 30 years. Presumably we are all expected to be able to drive to some more salubrious place when in need.

Some 50 years ago Fred H. Crossley wrote how Middlewich: 'has suffered severely at the hands of the road surveyor, the sanitary inspector and those meddlesome people whose one idea of improvement is to destroy everything of age or interest.' The same meddlesome people have been even more active since then in all parts of

Cheshire. I only found one public urinal (without other facilities) and it was very neglected and ready for some public health official to condemn. It was in Birkenhead and had been updated with a white glazed pottery dado and a drain. All the other corners had been blocked up with bricks to prevent their use, so that all liquid went in the right direction. Presumably, before the drain was added visitors arranged themselves around the walls. I also found a disused unroofed pub urinal by the Stamford Arms in Little Bollington, which was used as a tip but the smell revealed it was still occasionally in use. The lower part of all internal walls was drained so you were afforded some privacy in selecting where to stand.

Many early urinals had walls with the lower portion covered in waterproof slate, including the partitions between standing spaces. Probably this was the origin of the term 'stones' for such places. The 1887 catalogue of the Twyford's company shows most of the varieties of urinal still in use today. I remember using an unusual contraption at the old Weaver Navigation School in Winsford. It was made of thick slate but was rather like a trough with a front about a foot high. Was this simply to prevent splashing your shoes? I have read of a similar thing filled with peat but this one had a drain and was full of fag ends. Schoolboys found urinals irresistible for smoking out of the teachers' way.

From Henry Walker, who used to live in Runcorn, comes this delightful memory of what I guess must have been the 'Flapper Election' of 1929 when women over 21 voted for the first time. Keen to get their vote a prospective male candidate declared, 'What we need in our streets are urinals for women.' Now that would have been equal opportunities indeed – I bet they wouldn't have been allowed to demolish them either!

An almost vanished street scene – the entrance to a urinal at Birkenhead. The iron structure on the wall to the right once had an ornamental light and you turned a corner on entering so no one could see inside. It has no roof so the rain can cleanse it from time to time.

A boy at a Middlewich chemical works popped outside for an emergency call. However, he chose a corner where electrical equipment had been placed – and it was still connected. He went home with more than his pride injured.

An old Liverpool Rag Mag provided this gem:

> (Overheard in Birkenhead)
> Visitor: 'Where will I find the urinal?'
> Docker: 'Try Cammel Laird; they do all the big ships.'

[8]

SIXTY GLORIOUS YEARS ON THE THRONE

This was the motto for Queen Victoria's Diamond Jubilee in 1897 and it seems appropriate, as the main developments in creating the modern lavatory system took place in her time. It was prompted by events such as the cholera epidemic of 1830 (which spread as a result of foul cesspits and drains) and typhus outbreaks. Typhus killed the Prince Consort and was traced to 52 cesspits under Windsor Castle, and it also nearly killed the Prince of Wales after a visit to a Yorkshire house with faulty drains. Pioneers of medicine and public health slowly improved conditions, but half a century after Albert died many places were still little better served. Much of the development is reflected in and around Cheshire.

Indeed part of Cheshire was converted from a swamp by the refuse from its neighbouring city of Manchester. The content of all the privies there could not possibly be disposed of in the city, and some was sold to Cheshire farmers for next to nothing as 'Manchester manure'. Yet there was plenty left. The solution was the 'shit barges' which were filled in the city and taken to the 'shit wharfs' at Bollington and other places on the Bridgewater Canal. There the contents were loaded into little trains which ran on tracks raised on cinders and ashes from Manchester. What had been Carrington Moss, and too dangerous to walk on, was slowly converted to agricultural land and the former railways became the straight roads of those parts.

The 19th century saw a rapid growth in new industrial towns in the county, a process which has continued into the present century and former villages like Weaverham or

Holmes Chapel are large residential areas today. Places which were only hamlets when Victoria came to the throne were major boroughs by the time she died. This sudden growth of population caused all sorts of problems with the need for the provision of clean water for drinking and washing and the flushing of the waste. In Burnley and Manchester I saw simple privies which were just a room big enough for a seat built out from the backs of houses over the river behind, into which waste fell through a hole in the floor. Old paintings of Stockport viaduct show similar privies cantilevered over the Mersey. The privy has not altogether vanished from Stockport and the writer was able to advise on the reconstruction of one for the town's new Hatting Museum. Along the northern boundary from Birkenhead to Mottram, from Widnes to Winsford and along the moorland fringes of the east, rows of terraced houses were built around factories belching smoke, most of which had little if any facilities for disposing of waste other than burying it or putting it into the rivers. The smell of the factories with unemptied privies and cesspools was one of the most often described features of such places. No wonder country estate owners tried to create their own little utopias in rural Cheshire and the countryside became a Mecca for the well to do from the industrial cities and towns.

Birkenhead was the first new settlement; as the Mersey ferry system improved it was seen as a pleasant place to cross over to in order to spend some time in the new Regency fashion of sea bathing. This function was taken over later by the **New** Brighton which never achieved the popularity of the place it was named after. Birkenhead's nature was to change when Laird opened up the docks and amongst other 'firsts' it claimed flats, tramways and the public park and it was acknowledged as the first authority to ensure that every property had ample windows, ventilation and – significantly – sufficient privy provision. It could do this because right from the start officials took care to approve only superior development on what was hitherto a 'greenfields site'. People who visited (even Disraeli) could not help but comment on this as a vision of the future ideal, as it was unknown elsewhere in the country.

But Crewe was soon to equal it. Building started in the 1840s; as neither Winsford nor Nantwich wanted the railway junction so a new town was developed in open fields. There the LNWR company provided everything, including work, churches, social functions, a park (on land that the rival Midland Railway wanted to develop to keep them away), houses and of course privies which were ample and efficiently emptied into the Valley Brook each week by men employed by the company.

The company village became a feature of Victorian industry and some of the finest examples are in Cheshire. At Bromborough Pool, Price's Candle Factory set up a workers' colony in short rows of terraced houses with a village hall and allotments for vegetable production. When I turned off to visit I noticed someone had painted out the first 'L' from Pool Lane – which looked promising. Pevsner in his book on the buildings of Cheshire reports that the houses had internal water closets from the start in 1853. I think this is the only time that he even mentions such things! They must have been some of the first – if not the first – workers' cottages to have such luxury. Some flushing closets had been shown at the Great Exhibition of 1851 – where small potatoes, sponges and sheets of paper were used for demonstration purposes – and this was probably an influence. In the school yard there is what must be the most splendid school toilet block in Cheshire. Made of rusticated sandstone it resembles a small

The most impressive school toilets in Cheshire, resembling a little fort, at Bromborough Pool. The boys went to one side, the girls to the other and all was shielded by a rusticated sandstone wall.

fort with boys' and girls' facilities back to back surrounded by a stone privacy wall entered by an arch. A small tower contains the water-tank to provide gravity for flushing. It dates from 1898.

Only a mile away William Lever (later Lord Leverhulme) created his wonderful village of Port Sunlight, dedicated to clean and hygienic living. He decided that there should be a bathroom next to the front door of each house so that workmen could remove their work-clothes, take a bath and put on clean clothes for the evening. Privies, which were always WCs here too, were to be in a separate building at least 7 feet from the back door. They still survive in little rows of paired coal house and privy. Each privy has a single tile in the roof replaced by a thick pane of frosted glass to provide light and to prevent anyone peeping. The smallest toilet I found is in the model of a Port Sunlight house displayed in the Heritage Centre.

A splendid vista of privies at Port Sunlight. Lord Leverhulme specified that they had to be at least 7 feet from the back door and they were illuminated by a frosted glass tile in the roof.

Knutsford Gaol must have had enviable 'en suite' facilities for the time, for when it was remodelled in the 1850s each cell had a single bed and a flushing WC. The water was raised from a well underneath and pumped to tanks in the roof by the most awkward of prisoners who were set to turn the treadmill, making their punishment of use to the rest. It flowed from there to all parts by gravity.

Not every development used flushing toilets. The Winnington works of Brunner Mond were developed near Northwich, which had terrible problems with providing water and removing sewage because continual subsidence caused by salt extraction simply split the pipes open. Their solution when they started to provide houses was invented, originally making use of earth, by the Rev Henry Moule of Dorset only four years before the factory was built. The

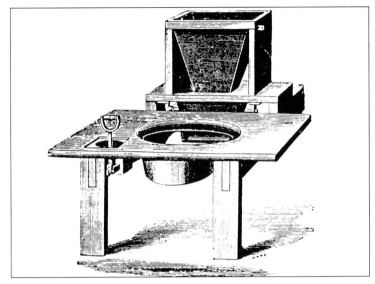

Reverend Henry Moule's 'pull-up' earth closet of 1860.

Winnington version was a metal contraption which fitted around the tub but where modern flushing toilets have a cistern it had a metal container for ashes. After use a lever was activated and a measure of ash was deposited into the tub. The factory produced plenty of ashes, so a supply was always available and they were delivered through a small door at chest height in the back alleyways. They continued in use until after the Second World War and the men who delivered the factory ashes and emptied the tubs were exempted from war service to prevent Winnington overflowing.

The enquiries into the provision of water for Northwich reveal much about conditions around 100 years ago. While some came from wells a large portion was taken from Wade Brook which was fed by other streams into which raw sewage

The small door in this back wall at Winnington was for delivery of ash from the works into the hopper of a Moule's closet which delivered a layer of ash after each visit to the privy.

emptied (see chapter 5), while along its banks were farms with manure heaps, pigsties and shippons and each had a cesspool, one of which was overflowing. Houses in the Rural District emptied their sewers directly into it and outbreaks of typhus had been traced to origins there. Although the experts stated that the water was unfit to drink it was similar to that in other places. In Victorian times, for example, much of Stockport was supplied by water taken from the heavily polluted River Mersey. It was stated at another Northwich enquiry that there were 262 cesspools and 1,543 pail closets in 1914. 'Not only is there the inconvenience of emptying them but there is no proper and convenient place into which the contents can be put.' It was a problem that was only partly solved by the installation of the sewage pumping station in a little castelated turret by the railway arches. This can be visited on certain days in the summer.

An 1899 committee into the housing of the working class, chaired by Richard Harding Watt (the builder of Knutsford's fantasy houses in Legh Road) was informed that in Knutsford there were:

```
Houses with water closets . . . . . . . . . . . . . . . 69
   "      "    Duckett's closets  . . . . . . . . . . . . 24
   "      "    handflushed closets  . . . . . . . . 102
               (buckets or bowls of water
               were poured down)
   "      "    pails  . . . . . . . . . . . . . . . . . . . . . 25
   "      "    peat pails  . . . . . . . . . . . . . . . . . 16
   "      "    earth closets . . . . . . . . . . . . . . . 9
   "      "    privies . . . . . . . . . . . . . . . . . . . 250
   "      "    cesspools  . . . . . . . . . . . . . . . . 11
   "      without sanitary conveniences . . . . 76
```

There were 152 houses that did not have their own independent conveniences.

John Henry Cooke, who was appointed Clerk to the Local Board of Health in 1875, recorded: 'Winsford at that time had no public water supply and was not sewered or lighted and the footpaths were not formed or paved. People used to carry hand lanterns at night in the streets and got their water from a public pump . . . There were cesspits and privies in abundance. A water-closet was unknown. There had been many deaths from Cholera in 1866.' The later cholera of 1888 was traced to labourers from the Continent. They had been recruited from Liverpool (where they had been stranded without enough money to continue their emigration to America) to break the strike of salt workers. They were crammed, regardless of age or sex, into rooms where many would sleep together on the floor in the only clothes they had. The cholera germs multiplied in the totally inadequate and overflowing cesspits. Cholera had first arrived from India, where it is endemic, in 1830 and soon spread to Northwich on the salt boats. There the damaged and inadequate sewers made an ideal home. In 1884 the costs of scavengers (nightsoil men) in Winsford for the year was £62, while the foreman received £3 13s 4d a year.

At Queen Victoria's Diamond Jubilee banquet in Northwich a Winsford official caused outrage by drawing attention to the foul drinking water they were served. At one held in Winsford the speakers referred to the sewage works. Not the usual after dinner topic, it must be admitted. They were very proud of their facilities as there was a filter-bed on either side of the river, by the appropriately named 'Bottom Flash', to serve both sides of the town. Lord Delamere, the first UDC Chairman, had suggested that they used the basses (compacted flame resistant waste from the fires at the salt works) for filtration. The basses made ideal homes for the microbes and Winsford developed a small industry exporting them as far as Yorkshire. The local children were not bothered by the technicalities but broke down the fences to get at the tomatoes and cucumbers which seeded naturally in the filter beds.

Not every town was so well provided for and those which developed from market towns into huge industrial ones suffered most. A report on Macclesfield's public health in 1849 stated: 'The drains are neither water nor air tight, a continual soakage goes on, rendering the internal walls damp and emitting noxious effluvia.' As late as 1876 Stockport had 'houses surrounded by swamps of sludge, slops and other offensive matter, resulting from a want of drainage and privy accommodation.' People had to make their way on planks, old doors and blocks of wood.

In the cotton and silk mills of East Cheshire provision for the

The 'necessary' towers behind Quarry Bank Mill, Styal. Each contained a privy with nothing more than a hole in the floor – six, one above the other – until 1902, when the bridging section at the top was built to provide the ventilated entrance the law required and bucket privies. (Courtesy of Quarry Bank Mill Trust)

workers was essential. Some of the mills still have a tower on the outside wall containing a stairway and a privy on each floor. However, at Quarry Bank Mill, Styal, now a prize property of the National Trust, a fascinating story is preserved in the factory accounts. At the rear of the tall mill building there are four turrets, each providing a privy on each floor. One original early 19th-century example survives untouched and is simply a circular hole in the sandstone floor of a small cubicle. I guess there might have been some form of simple seat to prevent people falling down, but the faeces fell through the holes in the floor on all six floors – one directly above the next – to be disposed of by the water flowing from the water wheels. This situation satisfied everyone – or if it didn't (especially if someone used the one

A bucket privy at Quarry Bank Mill, Styal, provided after the woman factory inspector's visit in 1902, to comply with the Factory Acts. (Courtesy of Quarry Bank Mill Trust)

above where they were sitting), they couldn't do much about it! 'A woman factory inspector' arrived in 1902 and was appalled. She pointed to the law that employees must not go direct into a works privy but had to get to it through a ventilated passage. The solution? One privy was used as the entrance and the space between it and the next tower was bridged over, with a small opening for ventilation at head height. A bucket privy was installed and these were in use until the mill ceased to function just before the Second World War. The village of Styal impressed many visitors for its conditions and facilities which were far more pleasant and healthy than those in the cities and towns. The Greg family who provided the houses were proud that each dwelling had a privy with a cistern for flushing water. They can still be seen today.

Styal has a lot in common with the country estates of the titled families. The Duke of Westminster's Deeside villages had excellently designed outbuildings by John Douglas, including privies. There are splendid arrays of pigsties and privies behind most of the houses on the Peckforton Estate. At Bostock, where an oak tree marks the traditional centre of Cheshire, each cottage had a small privy and pigsty unit, which still stand though they were replaced by flushing toilets years ago. Until this year when mains water was provided they had relied on water raised from a well by a windmill and stored in a tower above the old village laundry building. An interesting roadside feature outside the laundry (now the village hall) is a tall pipe as high as a lamp-post with a crown top to stop birds nesting in it. This was to allow foul and explosive gasses to escape from the drains. Such features were once common but are currently removed for 'safety' by local councils.

I was particularly interested in Rostherne, an estate village

This is the best photo I could get of the profusion of privies, coal houses and ash stores behind the cottages at Rostherne because of the mottled light caused by the trees.

where some houses were built to replace the former village in Tatton Park. The houses were said to have been constructed without back doors as Lady Egerton believed that gossip spread over back fences. I wondered what facilities I would find there. I first went to the square of houses that I was told had only front doors, but found each with a back door leading into a yard with a former privy. The walls were far too high to gossip over and several had been given a roof of corrugated iron or plastic to make serviceable extra rooms. Perhaps it was the high walls which gave rise to the story about gossips. Over the road were outbuildings of the pigsty and privy variety, while further down the lane was a whole block with privies, coal houses with low doors, and roofed shelters where ashes for the privy were once stored, now used for the dustbins.

There were other problems facing the Victorians. The traditional parish church was almost always next to an inn where people could call in and use the facilities besides getting refreshments after the services. The early Nonconformist churches had to be built at least five miles from the nearest church, but after the Toleration Act of 1689 they were allowed to build in the towns. The Methodists provided chapels in rural areas to serve farming communities who might travel for a long distance, as did the visiting preacher. As Methodists they could not pop into pubs – often there wasn't one handy anyway – and so most chapels had their own privies. They have mostly been upgraded with flushing facilities inside. However, at Bradley I came upon a tiny chapel which had the inscription 'POOR MAN'S BETHEL' above the door. There was a small, long-disused privy joined to a stable and carriage shed – probably for the minister – next to the chapel, with its entrance behind a wooden privacy screen.

This little structure in the school yard at Edge provided a stable for the teacher's horse with an entrance on the front. To the side, behind a modesty screen, was a privy for all the pupils at this one-roomed school near the Welsh border.

Other needs arose. Following the Education Acts large numbers of schools were developed. Most older people remember their outside toilets – some simple tubs, others which were automatically flushed, as I described in chapter 6. I spotted a few disused outside toilets in school playgrounds and found a lovely little privy for all the pupils and staff built into the stable for the teacher's horse outside the tiny one-roomed school at Edge, which is now used as a nursery. It is Government policy that there should no longer be outside toilets for any school, so another reminder of the past is disappearing – though I don't expect the children will regret that!

[9]

GOING POTTY

Pottery had always been used for chamber pots as it was light and could be rinsed easily, but for moving a week's produce from a household it was too fragile. It was only when drains and sewers became available so that the container could stay put, along with kilning methods to cope with large pieces easily, that it became the usual material to sit on.

The modern day successor to such famous names as Twyford's, Doulton's and Crapper (who else) is Caradon who now operates Europe's biggest factory producing bathroom fittings (a nice modern euphemism) at Alsager, giving the story a place in a Cheshire book. It was built between 1956 and 1958 and has been added to since. Its reception block contains a delightful gallery housing the collection of water closets and lavatorial odds and ends excellently displayed – as attractive as an art gallery – and the craftsmanship is excellent. Serious students can make arrangements to study there but for security reasons it is not open to the general public. A wide range of water closets, richly decorated with moulded embellishment or transfer prints, is on show along with a host of other devices including commode pans, bidets set in stools, urine bottles, sinks, a bath and even holders for cut up newspaper.

There had been flushing toilets of one sort or another since Queen Elizabeth's godson, Sir John Harington, invented one which was so complicated that it needed the instructions in a book hanging by the side. There is a slight Cheshire link, for the family later owned Gawsworth Hall. There was little point

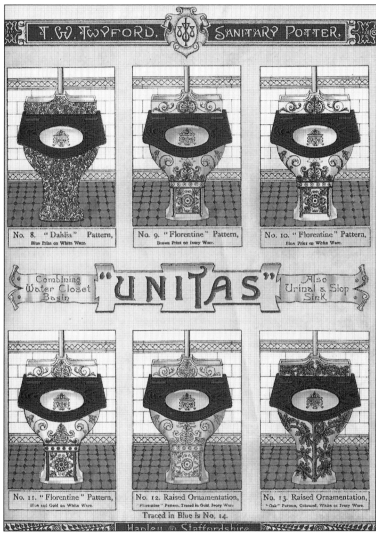

Varieties of elegance, illustrations of the sorts of designs that could be printed or moulded onto Twyford's Unitas with its special holder for paper behind the seat, from the 1888 catalogue. Surely there must still be a market for decorated loos?

in developing flushing toilets for general use until there were
efficient drains to carry the contents away. The first glazed,
and therefore waterproof, pipes for these were provided in
1842 by Doulton's (whose sanitary ware section is now
merged into Caradon).

Many people believe that Thomas Crapper invented the
modern lavatory. He did not invent the seating portion but
he patented the system of valves and syphons in the cistern,
which ensured that only the amount of water needed was
released each time the chain was pulled. Previously, flushing
depended on a variety of taps which could be left running.
Most Victorian houses were not connected to the mains so
well water had to be pumped to a tank in the loft from which
it flushed by gravity. A tap carelessly left on could drain it
completely. The EEC has decided that Britain can no longer
exclude the far simpler, though wasteful, Continental
cisterns and by the time this book reaches you Crapper's
superior cisterns will no longer be standard. The term
'Crapper' became fairly general for any flushing toilet in the
same way as Biro for a pen even though other manufacturers
introduced their own versions. However, the use of the word
'crap' in association with lavatories goes back hundreds of
years and is derived from the Roman god Crepitus who
presided over the digestive system. Crapper left his name for
us to see locally, cast into a drain cover in the courtyard at
Dunham Massey where he must have provided a lavatory,
though no records are known.

A variety of pottery seating facilities, with varying degrees of
efficiency, were tried in Victorian times but most came in
parts so that there were joints – ideal places for germs to
breed. Thomas Twyford of Hanley in the Potteries had
manufactured variants on the 'Bramah' which had been
used since the 18th century. He had sold over 100,000 of his

'National' version by 1888. In it water flowed into a bowl and was washed by a flush from behind into a pipe at the front (which acted as a urinal). He invented the 'Unitas' (patented in 1885) which was the first to combine the modern S or P water trap to prevent smells etc from coming up the drains with an efficient rim to flush all round the bowl and a small pool of water to keep the bottom clean. A Unitas seat with Crapper's cistern above it was the high-point of Victorian efficiency and has remained standard to the present day with only small changes to the shape but not the function.

However Caradon is not the only company making water closets in Cheshire. With the Ideal Standard factory on the Trent and Mersey Canal at Cledford, near Middlewich, the county probably produces more of them than anywhere else. Indeed, whenever you sit on a modern lavatory there is a fair chance that it came from Cheshire.

WARTIME COMFORT

At Stockport the air-raid shelters which were excavated to provide up to 7,000 places in the soft sandstone under the town in the Second World War were mostly below the main drainage. Near the entrance, however, is a section with large saltglazed earthenware drains on each side. At intervals there is a circular hole in the pipe with wooden sections of a seat on each side securely held in place. A tank was filled regularly and flushed to carry the contents away to the main sewer at that level. They are standard units and similar facilities using the same method were provided in military or refugee camps throughout the War. As the tunnels were expanded the engineers followed the Home Office guidelines of one chemical toilet for every 25 persons in short tunnels between the larger ones. They were felt to be

Even when the Blitz threatened, people had to answer the call of nature. This drain with seats on top was provided for those sheltering in the air-raid tunnels at Stockport. There were partitions of canvas or tarred paper and a sacking 'door'.

more likely to survive an air-raid than shelters with sewers.

There were no solid partitions, only tarred paper nailed to upright timbers and no doors, either, only sheets of hessian which were used as wrapping for cotton bales and could be obtained secondhand from the mills. The Corporation were urged to fit doors but declined as so many people of both sexes were gathered together, declaring 'much more might happen behind a closed door than would be the case if they were open for supervisory purposes'. There had been a similar situation in the cotton mills where the privies only had partial doors or a sacking cover to the entrance to prevent people wasting time by smoking or just sitting in them.

LONG LIVE THE PRIVY!

Chemical toilets were provided in the underground nuclear bunker at Hack Green near Nantwich which was away from the main sewers and would be too deep for them anyway – presumably they would survive a holocaust and still be serviceable while sewers might not.

Perhaps this book will come in handy, if it survives a future conflagration and people have to return to basics again!

AND FINALLY . . .

Cheshire is well known for its peat bogs and the famous bog body 'Lindow Man' or 'Pete Marsh' was found in one near Wilmslow in 1984. When this book was being prepared, a letter to the *Winsford Chronicle* noted the resemblance between the reconstructed Lindow Man and the author, commenting that both were associated with bogs. So far, no relationship between these two bog men has been established!

Paying a Call – Some Places to Visit

Most of the privies that I have included are in private properties and so their location has been left vague to avoid people making unwanted calls on the owners. However, in and around Cheshire there are some places open to the public with lavatorial interest. Please check that they are open before you set out to avoid a wasted journey as some have seasonal openings.

BEESTON CASTLE: wardrobe tower with privies – one in a window – by the gatehouse. Telephone: 01829 260464.

BOAT MUSEUM, Ellesmere Port; privy (with occupant) and boatmen's chamber pots. Telephone: 0151 355 5017.

DUNHAM MASSEY, Altrincham: NT property with two fine close stools. Telephone: 0161 941 1025.

GLADSTONE POTTERY MUSEUM, Stoke on Trent: excellent collection of lavatorial ceramics. Telephone: 01782 311378.

GREATER MANCHESTER MUSEUM OF SCIENCE AND INDUSTRY: gallery devoted to sewers and associated topics. Telephone: 0161 832 2244.

LITTLE MORETON HALL, south of Congleton: privy tower and privy in magnificent Tudor mansion. Telephone: 01260 272018.

NORTHWICH: Edwardian Sewage Pumping Engine, in small building next to the river. Telephone: 01257 260157.

NORTON PRIORY, near Runcorn: an excavated reredorter and magnificent drain. Telephone: 0192 8569895.

QUARRY BANK MILL, Styal: privy towers at 18th-century cotton mill (NT). Telephone: 01625 527468.

STOCKPORT AIR RAID SHELTERS: guided tours include viewing of elementary provision for use in wartime. Telephone: 0161 480 1940.

STOCKPORT: in preparation – privy behind reconstructed hatter's cottage. Telephone: 0161 480 2922.

TWYFORD'S, Alsager (Caradon Bathrooms): gallery of company products containing splendid historic collection (appointment only). Telephone: 0270 879777.